Character Education

Respect

by Lucia Raatma

Consultant:
Madonna Murphy, Ph.D.
Associate Professor of Education,
University of St. Francis, Joliet, Illinois
Author, *Character Education in America's Blue Ribbon Schools*

Bridgestone Books
an imprint of Capstone Press
Mankato, Minnesota

Bridgestone Books are published by Capstone Press
818 North Willow Street, Mankato, Minnesota 56001
http://www.capstone-press.com

Library of Congress Cataloging-in-Publication Data
Raatma, Lucia.
  Respect/by Lucia Raatma.
    p. cm.—(Character education)
  Includes bibliographical references (p. 24) and index.
  Summary: Describes respect as a virtue and suggests ways in which
children can recognize and practice being respectful.
    ISBN 0-7368-0371-8
  1. Respect for persons—Juvenile literature. 2. Conduct of life—Juvenile
literature. [1. Respect.] I. Title. II. Series.
BJ1533.R42R23 2000
177'.1—dc21   99-29178
                                                                          CIP

Editorial Credits
Damian Koshnick, editor; Heather Kindseth, cover designer and illustrator;
  Kimberly Danger, photo researcher

Photo Credits
Corbis, 18
David F. Clobes, 16
Photo Network/Amy Lundstrom, cover; bachmann, 14
Photri-Microstock/FOTOPIC, 20
Shaffer Photography/James L. Shaffer, 8
Unicorn Stock Photos/Eric R. Berndt, 4; Jeff Greenberg, 10
Uniphoto/Jackson Smith, 6
Visuals Unlimited/Cheryl A. Ertelt, 12

Table of Contents

Respect

Respect is believing in the worth of others. Respect means treating others as you want to be treated. Respecting others means considering their needs and feelings. For example, you respect others' needs when you are quiet in a library.

worth
the quality that makes someone or something important

Respecting Yourself

Respecting yourself means taking care of your needs. It means paying attention to your mind, your body, and your feelings. Brushing your teeth is an example of respecting your body. Studying in school shows you respect your mind.

Respecting Your Family

Being respectful of your family shows that you care about them. You can show respect for your mom by asking how her day went. You also can show respect by saying thank you. For example, thank your dad when he helps you clean your room.

Respecting Your Friends

Respecting your friends means treating them as you want them to treat you. Respect is asking when you want to use a friend's toy. It is listening while your friend is talking. Respect means helping friends when they ask for help.

Respect through Sports

Respecting the rules of a game is important. It also is important to respect other players. Respectful people do not complain when they lose to another team. Respect is trying the best you can for yourself and for your teammates.

complain
to say you are unhappy
about something

Respect at School

You can show respect in school by being polite. For example, you can raise your hand before you speak. You can be on time to the bus stop. Being polite shows that you care about others.

polite
having good manners; being kind and thoughtful.

Respecting Others' Belongings

You can show respect by treating other people's toys well. For example, put a friend's bicycle in a safe place so it will not be stolen. Taking care of other people's things shows that you value those people.

"I hope that children today will grow up without hate. I hope they will learn to respect one another, no matter what color they are."
–Rosa Parks

Respect and Rosa Parks

Rosa Parks is an African American woman who believes in equal rights. In 1955, Rosa chose not to give her bus seat to a white man. This made people think about laws that were unfair to African Americans. Rosa fought for the respect that all people deserve.

Respect and You

Respect is about appreciating the people and things in your life. Showing respect is important for making friends. Other people will respect you if you respect them.

appreciate
to enjoy or value something
or someone

21

▼ Hands On: Make a Respect Collage

Learn about respect by finding pictures that show people being respectful.

What You Need

Scissors
Construction paper
Glue
Magazines

What You Do

1. Look through magazines.
2. Find and cut out pictures that show respect.
3. Paste your pictures onto a piece of construction paper.
4. Explain to your friends how each picture shows respect.

Ask your friends to make their own collages. Talk with your friends about how their pictures show respect.

Words to Know

belonging (bee-LONG-ing)—something that someone owns

consider (kuhn-SID-ur)—to think about something

deserve (di-ZURV)—to earn something because of the way you act

polite (puh-LITE)—having good manners; being kind and thoughtful.

worth (WURTH)—the quality that makes someone or something important

Read More

Goley, Elaine P. *Learn the Value of Respect.* Vero Beach, Fla.: Rourke, 1988.

Kaufman, Gershen and Lev Raphael. *Stick Up For Yourself!* Every Kid's Guide to Personal Power and Positive Self-Esteem. Minneapolis: Free Spirit, 1990.

Internet Sites

Adventures from the Book of Virtues Home Page
http://www.pbs.org/adventures/
Character Building Site
http://www.usoe.k12.ut.us/curr/char_ed/chbldr/character builder.html
Character Counts!
http://www.charactercounts.org/index.htm

Index